Karum Singh Cheema

POETIC GIBBERISH

Where Chaos Meets Beauty

AUSTIN MACAULEY PUBLISHERS®
LONDON * CAMBRIDGE * NEW YORK * SHARJAH

Copyright © Karum Singh Cheema 2025

The right of Karum Singh Cheema to be identified as author of this work has been asserted by the author in accordance with sections 77 and 78 of the Copyright, Designs and Patents Act 1988.

All rights reserved. No part of this publication may be reproduced, stored in a retrieval system, or transmitted in any form or by any means, electronic, mechanical, photocopying, recording, or otherwise, without the prior permission of the publishers.

Any person who commits any unauthorised act in relation to this publication may be liable to criminal prosecution and civil claims for damages.

A CIP catalogue record for this title is available from the British Library.

ISBN 9781035880546 (Paperback)
ISBN 9781035880553 (e Pub e-book)

www.austinmacauley.com

First Published 2025
Austin Macauley Publishers Ltd®
1 Canada Square
Canary Wharf
London
E14 5AA

To every soul on their journey through life, regardless of the stage, be it in the midst of struggle, the process of healing, or navigating the uncertainties in between, this book is dedicated to you. Your resilience, your tenacity, and your unwavering spirit to keep moving forward inspire the world.

To my beloved family, your endless support, encouragement, and belief in me have been my guiding light. Your love fuels my journey every step of the way.

To my partner, your patience, understanding, and enduring love, especially during my most challenging moments, have been my anchor. I'm grateful for your support even when I've been hard to love.

A special thank you to my higher self and the divine for being my guiding force through life's trials. Your presence and guidance through the hardships have been my saving grace. You've kept me strong and alive.

Thank you all for being a part of this journey. Your presence, love, and support are cherished beyond words.

Contents Page

There's no roadmap to the mind, no neatly labelled chapters that compartmentalise our thoughts. Life moves in a constant, unbroken stream, and in this collection, *Poetic Gibberish*, it embraces that fluidity.

In the absence of chapters and a contents page, these poems echo the randomness of our thoughts, each verse a spontaneous reflection of life's chaos and splendour. There's no sequence to dictate the order, no prescribed path to follow; instead, it's an exploration of moments, emotions, and musings as they naturally unfold.

Dive into a world without structure, where the absence of order is the canvas for genuine expression.

As you dive into this book, you'll notice some "Random Thought Questions" scattered among the poems. These are little prompts to ponder over, meant to stir your thoughts and feelings. They're like little nudges to explore your own thoughts and feelings while reading.

An Inspirational Prelude

'To live is to suffer but to survive is to find meaning in the suffering.'

—Friedrich Nietzsche [Philosopher]

I remember that moment vividly—sitting in my uncle's car, a struggling teenager lost in a world of thoughts, when I first heard DMX's song *Slippin*. Instantly, the quote that echoed through the song gripped me and changed my perspective. In that moment, the song became more than just music; it became a lifeline, a coping mechanism that has stayed with me to this day. I'll forever be thankful for that transformative moment, for the strength it provided in my darkest hours.

This Nietzsche quote, intertwined with DMX's powerful lyrics, became a philosophy I applied to navigate my own challenges, providing strength and direction. It wasn't just a Nietzsche quote; it became a part of me, a guiding light through life's turmoil. As I share these words with you, I hope they offer the same solace, strength, and guidance they've provided me. A heartfelt thank you and rest in peace to DMX. And a special thank you to my uncle, who introduced me to DMX and opened my world to this profound influence.

I hope this helps you on your healing journey

The Key Within

Surrender to yourself,
And set you free,
Only you hold the key.

Scattered Thoughts

Scattered thoughts on a blank canvas,
Paint the best pictures.

Hard to know what is what,
But the heart can understand.

Poetic gibberish rolls off the tongue.

A mind full of lessons,
A heart full of stone.

Born Into War

Trauma is a stray bullet that caught
you in the crossfire

Yet you must heal yourself
Armour up

And fight in an everlasting war that
wasn't yours

Framed Innocence

Sometimes I look at my baby pictures and talk to them,
For I wish I could go back and give myself what I was deprived of,
the love, the laughter, the reassurance,
A part of me wishes I could reach into the image,
and hold the soul as if I know everything that child is going to go through,
just to cry with them,
laugh with them,
and hold them as if I'm freeing them of any future pain,
But if I take that pain away,
the person holding this photo wouldn't be who they are today.

Pulled Out from the Roots

The mother tongue forcefully cut from our mouths.
Or did we fail to stick up for ourselves?
Born on foreign land,
But home roots stay embedded deep within.

How did we get so distant from our motherland?
Failing to know we have the blood of warriors running through our veins,
Knowledge of our ancestors vanishes along with our elders,
As the barriers between communication prevent us from sharing common ground.

So many questions we want to ask,
But we're lost for words.
So many stories we want to hear,
But fail to open the book.

We can sit back and blame our surroundings,
But the truth is it's all within us.
We live and breathe it,
Yet fail to channel it,
So disconnected with our bloodline.

But I won't die with regret,
For I will recover lost history.
And bring my soul back to the soil where it was formed,
And connect with the divine that's within.
To bring me closer to my people, my language,
My history, my land.

ME vs Me

Stuck in the belief of my
own delusions

Contradicting what I know
to be fact

The minds a powerful weapon

The cause of my demise

Soul Connected Strangers

I know we've never met,
Or we've never spoken,
But when I saw you,
Our souls conversated,
And like old friends, they rejoiced,
A connection that goes back many lifetimes,
Felt reignited deep within,
A whole lifetime flashed by,
It felt like I knew you forever,
But in reality,
I guess we are just soul-connected strangers.

Home Beneath the Surface

Rock bottom is a thing of beauty,
The jagged edges of the surface,
The illusion of a way out,
The light within the darkness,
Forever feels like you're falling,
Even when you're climbing,
The eerie whispers of the mind echoing in this bottomless pit.

Through time this pit became a home,
A home that I no longer want to escape,
As I outgrew it,
The same home that once tied me down,
Set me free,
The same home I hated,
Ruthlessly nurtured me,
I didn't know I needed it until that time passed,
And I forever look back at that bottomless pit,
As the master and I the student,
The artist and I the art,
The home that I needed in that moment in time,
The answers for all my success,
The change that I needed to grow,
A place within my heart that'll forever be a home.

Sharpening Pencils

I miss the simple times,
Sharpening pencils by the bin,
Not a worry in the world.

Until We Meet Again

If we could speak again,
I'd tell you how much I love you.
If I could see you again, I'd just hug you,
If I could hold you again, I'd never let go.
I wish I'd done these things before you left,
But time doesn't wait for anyone.
So, one last time I kiss you,
Before I lay you to rest.

Captive of Safety

I stare at the keys while wearing these handcuffs,
Drowning in the comfort of safety.
For the known chill of steel speaks louder than the uncertain warmth of liberty.

Wasted Talent

Sunken dreams float to the surface
A reminder of what could've once been
Self-imposed restraints, resembling
Chains in confinement
Who or what I could've been
Only time could tell
My time is up
Yet I'm still trying to fathom
There's nothing worse on this planet
Than wasted talent

Random Thought

Is the villain really a villain?
 Or just a failed hero?

Lover's Death

I forgive you for piercing my heart with the blade of love.
I needed to be reborn.
Without you, this wouldn't have been possible.

I thank you for pushing me off the cliff of trust,
making me hit rock bottom.
For now, this place is a home forever in my heart.

I accept your non-existent apology as the words
Left unspoken, I found closure to heal my wounds.

Now that time has passed,
I think you should forgive yourself.
For when I look back, I see a lost soul screaming for help

By hurting me,
you only hurt yourself.

I forgive you.
You didn't know what you had.
I know my worth now,
and I promise I'll never come back.

A Broken Fix

Once lost, can trust be regained?
I think about this a lot.
Once something is broken,
No matter how much you repair it,
It'll never look exactly like it used to.

His and Hers Perspective

Female—Every time I look at him, I know I gave it my all.
Male—Every time I look at her, I know I could've given more.

I lost parts of myself in the process of love.
I took what I could in the process of lust.

I put his needs before mine.
I neglected how she felt most of the time.

His eyes would make all my worries go away.
Her eyes told stories of a thousand pains.

Is love always supposed to be this hard?
This one-way love can't function in the heart.

Ignoring the tears, I still forgive.
She deserves a man, not a kid.

As he lets me go a part of me dies.
I wasn't the one nor was it the right time.

I wish I knew to love you need thick skin.
I wish I knew that I had the change within.

The blooming blossoms now turned grey.
She's the biggest loss of my life, the one that got away.

How could I ever love the same?
How do I live with the regret of pain?

We part ways onto unknown paths.
Until it was gone, I never knew what I had.
Scarred by the changes I don't know how to trust.
It's too late to tell her it really was love.

He taught me what heartbreak was.
And she taught me how to love.

Backpack and My Path

This path is a lonely one,
but I wouldn't ask for it any other way.
Through the darkness I remain on this route,
for I know a light waits for me at the end of this journey.
I shall not give up hope nor look for shortcuts on this path,
for my path is created for me, by me and to lead me to my destiny.
I'm destined for greatness, and I will change the world,
and this journey all starts with my backpack and my path.

The Blind Eye

The blind eye sees all
Yet doesn't acknowledge

Tugging the Heart Strings

Trusting someone is like being connected to a rope
from one heart to another
A constant tug-of-war
Where one heart's strain often ends with the other's collapse

Portal to the Soul

The eyes are a portal to the soul
They speak a thousand words
But the story remains untold

Separate Peaks

Outgrowing someone you love can be so hard
It's like you can see the peak of the mountaintop
and they can't

As the love remains strong
you want to push them to continue climbing
But instead, it feels like you're dragging a lifeless
body uphill

Slowly it weights you down
causing you to slip
Is it selfish to cut the cord in order to reach the peak?
Or do you try and make them see what's in front of them?

I've tried to show them what I see
I've even allowed myself to gradually slip down the
mountain as they pulled me with them,
still trying to open their eyes to what's insight
But at what point do you stop?

You've worked so hard to climb to this point
yet you're allowing yourself to slip back to the bottom
of the mountain
due to wanting to finish what you started with someone
Some people can only make it to a certain level
It doesn't mean you're a bad person to continue to
climbing to the next
For you did your best to bring them this far with you

If anything, you cut out pieces of you
And tried placing them inside your loved one
Hoping to bring them back to life and keep climbing
but it doesn't work like that
You can still reach the top by yourself
And be the change you want them to see
Instead of trying to open their eyes

Call their name with love whilst you place your flag
on the peak of that mountain

If they truly love you back
They'll persevere through that journey
And join you at the top
And if they don't,
You'll be glad you cut the cord and climbed

Random Thought

How many times have you wanted to share your work, but hesitated, as you foresaw all the judgement and lost all belief in yourself?

Strangers from a Distance

Soft lips speak the harshest words
Said you'd stick by my side
Until you turned
Our Paths Crossed
Love got lost
Yet there are lessons learned
Strangers from a distance
But still, those memories burn

Be Present

The best advice I ever received was
"Be Present"
I brushed it off when I first heard the words
But when life tested me
For some reason, my mind said to be present

Trying to apply advice I never understood at first took time
But gradually with each inhale and exhale my mind became more present

I lived in the moment
Not worrying about what has happened or what's going to happen
I found more clarity
My mind more clear

I wasn't drowning in my thoughts anymore
I was appreciating the moment I was blessed to be experiencing

So, when I now feel myself slipping
I make sure to remind myself
To close my eyes
Deeply inhale

And exhale
And be present in the moment
For this moment will pass
And forever be a distant memory
That I wish I enjoyed

So why not enjoy it as it happens
Instead of replaying a recording in my head
Craving to feel the emotions I felt in that moment

Thank you to my brother Randeep for this advice

Isn't This What You Asked For?

The late nights
The hard work
The painful days
The moments that hurt
Isn't this what you asked for?

The mental tests
The physical stress
The loss of friends
The thoughts of giving in
Isn't this what you asked for?

You lose faith
You give, they take
Seeing no results
Thinking why am I doing this for?
Isn't this what you asked for?

To quit now would be a waste of talent
So, Trust the process
because in the end
it'll eventually happen,

To reap the rewards
you must endure
These hardships will craft you to take more

And if you stop
You'll be stuck thinking what could've
But if you don't
You'll be glad you never gave up

So, when you're feeling high
Or you feel like you can't take any more
Just remind yourself
This is what you asked for

Bamboo trees take 5 years to grow to their full potential. People with patience water them every day, even when no progress is shown for 5 years.

Other people think they're crazy for watering something that's not "growing."

The people watering the plant know that with patience and dedication, the tree will get to where they want.

Eventually after 5 years the bamboo tree grows and is up to 90ft tall. Once people see that bamboo trees reach over 90ft tall they'll say they never doubted you even though they called you crazy when you were watering it.

Think of watering the bamboo tree as chasing your dreams. You may have nothing to show for the progress but at the end of the day, you know what you want, and you know what you're chasing/ growing

Once people see your dream, or goal reach its destination that you had in mind they'll say they never doubted you.

Random Thought

What makes the more accurate
first judgement, the heart or
the mind.

Fr33doomed

Freedom is an illusion
In reality we believe that we are free
Yet we're doomed
Caged birds telling one another that we can fly
Yet choose to remain caged

Finding solace in illusion,
But never tasting authentic freedom,
Reveals our true state: FR33doomed.

Why do you hesitate to break the norm if you're free?
Why do you fear the consequences if you're free?
Why do you fear losing love or respect if you're free?
Question yourself,
Are you truly free
Or living the illusion

We are given choices because we are free
Yet there are limitations on our freedom?
We are subconsciously shackled by unseen hands
Mere puppets partaking in one big show

But we can't be surely?
For we are free
We can vote, speak, eat and live how we please
The power of illusion can make one into fr33.
Fracturing the mind, body and soul into being controlled
The power of illusion will make you go against your own eyes
for it has the power of you

Next time you question your freedom
Think are you really free?
Or are u FR33doomed

I See Her in You

Every time I see you; I see her in you
When you speak, I hear the knowledge of an
old soul
So, I smile as I know
I see her in you

The way you mask your battle scars
The way your eyes shine like stars
When you smile
I see her in you

The strength you hold

The harsh truths you've told
Even when you're mad at me
I see her in you

People like her were so rare and few
She may have gone
But she's never forgotten
As I will always see her in you

Frostbitten Heart

A cloudy mind as I look up at clear skies
Trying to piece my thoughts together
Before I let our love die
Seeing those tears drip down your face
Left a hole inside my heart
I promise as long as I breathe, we'll never be apart
To put you through all of this I have to ask myself why
How can I give up
before I even tried
Once you spoke those words
I came back to my senses
Starstruck,
Thinking how could I be so selfish
And I promise from that day forward
The love will overshadow that pain
And what you felt that day
You'll never feel again

A friend:
Tell me about it, man. Sometimes I feel like my lower self is winning and I hate it

Me:

Think of it like this: you're sculpting the best version of yourself. Each time you pray, train, read, or do something that gets you closer to your higher self, you're breaking away pieces of rock to sculpt yourself.

Every day we pick up the hammer and chisel and hit away at our future selves, who we want to sculpt ourselves to be.

Some days, we don't even pick it up, and that's where our lower self may seem like it's winning. But it's okay. We're all learning and growing, trying to be better. But we can never let the lower self-moments define us when we've been carving away at our future self way more than we've been putting energy into our lower self.

Embrace the lower self, acknowledge the lower self, make peace with the lower self. Without the lower self, you wouldn't appreciate the higher self.

The Puppet Master

For me, people would backstab their own blood
For me, people would kill without hesitation
For me people would lie without remorse

People protect me with their life
I make them fall in love at first sight
I control their every move
You could even say I bring them happiness

The problem with falling in love with me is
Everyone is after me
They won't stop till they have me
And they'll destroy anything in their way to get me

Without me there would be no purpose
Without me there would be no control
Without me there would be no crime

I'll lead you to your demise
And I'll still continue to outlive you
For I, a piece of paper has no loyalty to anyone
Yet, have control over everyone
$ee how long you can last without m€

The puppet master aka Money

The Caterpillar and the Butterfly

I treat every day as my last
For I am one of many lucky souls
Gifted a second chance at life

I lay there, a wasted talent
Left with so much unfulfilled potential

But it wasn't my time
For my purpose was not yet fulfilled
Although I survived,
The man I was before had died
And I reborn

The universe gave me life once again
A second shot to right my wrongs
I remain forever in debt
Promising to not stop till my purpose is fulfilled

This was my butterfly out the cocoon moment
The new me, the real me
For me it took death to be reborn
An extreme circumstance to awaken the ancient soul
within me

I'll forever cherish my near death
Although to me I died that day,
I never got a chance to say thank you,

Thank you to the old me for taking that sacrifice
So that I can be the change my bloodline needed

A situation doesn't define you,
How you handle it after
Speaks volumes about the person you are

Random Thought

If you met the person you are today,
Would they be a beneficial addition
to your circle?

The bridge between Mountains

My grandfather left his homeland
In pursuit of providing for his bloodline
A stranded child with only a matchstick to guide
him in this eclipse
Starting from scratch
with nothing but his bare hands
A foreigner on uncharted territory

He was the bridge between mountains
The one who wasn't scared to jump
A man ready to be a causality of war
A Martyr for love

I am a product of him
Standing on the foundations he built
Looking around at all of my family
And seeing the parts of his soul he lost
Living In each and every one of them

He made the ultimate sacrifice
His hands bled so mine could be clean
His back broke so mine didn't have to
He turned this uncharted land into a home
So that I didn't have to fight to stay

And yet, after all of that
He asks for nothing in return
We'll I promise these foundations you built will
continue to remain
As through me you'll live on
And so will our family name

Unmasked

How can we expect external substances to heal the internal pain
A quick fix to keep the door to the soul sealed
So that we never have to face the monster on the other side
Eventually, the drink wears off
The high comes down
And so, you're left to sit with yourself
Staring in the mirror,
You see the true monster you've been trying to escape from this whole time
so, we repeat the cycle
For the monster becomes an ally when given a mask to hide

Pause, take a deep breath.

Two Hearts Never Break the Same

You do the same thing expecting different results
You love someone who refuses to change
Still proceed to give them your heart
After sweeping up the pieces,
Hoping that they can somehow fix it
We can't mend another's broken heart
For two hearts never break the same
Only we know our own
Only we have the touch to heal it

Consumed by What I Consume

Consumed by what I consume
Yet stuck in this reality
A failed escape only made me numb to the effects
Losing the ability to feel only makes you feel more
Seduced by what destroys me
For the substance takes control
Pulling the strings for me, the puppet
In this never-ending puppet show

The Normality of Loss

When a loved one returns to the spirit world
Your world instantly stops
The echoes of your heartbeat bounce through empty hallways
Time freezes at that moment
Everything moves in slow motion

The smell of that moment stays embedded in your senses
The feeling, a bottled memorabilia of trauma stored within
The thoughts in your mind, finally come to a halt

As you walk out those doors
You're faced against a world of normality
In disbelief, you question how everyone continues their day
Catching eyes with strangers, oblivious to your loss
At that very moment, amongst the crowds of people
Is the one moment you truly feel alone

Random Thought

If you could see someone's energy, would you be more mindful of where you place yours?

We Are the Divine

The divine resides within us all
For we are all one
Our human bodies are merely a shell
To protect our soul
We are spiritual beings
Having a human experience
All connected by the same thread
Yet separated in so many ways
They want us to lack knowledge of self
For the strength we harbour is beyond their grasp
A strength that will continue to live as a myth
As we may never see the power we hold as one

Deep in the Basement of the Soul

Like a shovel, words dig up past emotions once buried deep
Forcing you to relive a feeling you had never wished to revisit
Transported to a place where trauma lies

Do you ever truly heal?
Or do we just learn to cope?
When relatable poetry is read
The old me resurrects
Reminding the new me
That we can never be separated

Searching for a Purpose

A corpse floating on a rock in space
Lost without its purpose
Spending every day alive
But never living
Existence is pain
Just waiting to be set free

(un)Healed

There's no secret recipe for self-healing.
The work is done when you dive deep within.
When you're ready to reverse engineer all your
beliefs, trauma and who you are.
A place where you corner off all your comfort zones.
A place where u avoid fighting your demons,
But to sit with them and speak.
You must understand your demons in order to grow
Most of us bury them within the depths of our souls,
forever avoiding the cold feelings of facing them.
If we face these demons, we begin to heal.
Only we can truly unlock our full potential.
By avoiding them, it's like having a key to a treasure chest,
but dying before opening it.
Forever being left to question,
what you could've found within

Enlightenment is not the finishing line
But the start

I'm Proud of You

I'm so proud of you
You fought many cold wars
Some victories sweet
Some bitter
You stood tall in an army of one

Your fragmented armour displays your service
You had every reason to quit
Yet you didn't give in
You didn't let your battle scars define you
Nor did you turn out a bitter causality of war

But instead, you saw the beauty in the art of war
The blessings of bleeding from time to time
The sweet essence of pain
The sacrifices needed to survive

Now look at you as you read this
Finally at peace with yourself
Nothing but gratitude and love
for everyone and everything around you
A silent warrior who walks amongst the earth
No longer seeks to fight, but love
Seeking to protect those who are a casualty to this war
The war of life

Insecure Reflections

I voice my aspirations, manifesting them into reality
You sharply cut them down before they bloom
Does my ambition spark fear within you?
Does it shine a light on your own inability to chase after what you desire?
Your lack of self-belief won't anchor mine
Your limitations aren't mine to bear
Find peace in healing your own wounds
Rather than casting shadows onto the paths of others

You Are the One

You are the one from your family here to break the cycle
You are the one brave enough to face your trauma
You are the one to put a stop to unhealthy patterns
You are the one to break the generational curse
You are the one who feels what others don't
You are the one who sees things differently
You are the one that's making change
You are the one that'll create a better life for your children
You can't stop now
You are the one

Your path is written for you.
You're currently where you
once wished you'd be
Give yourself some credit
What's meant for you, will always find you
The universe will put you through hardships,
punish you and try to break you to see
how badly you want it

Timeless

I'm 23 years old
My mind is one from an old age
My heart is the age of many lifetimes
My eyes show the pain of a thousand deaths
My soul is just a visitor on this planet
For my time is temporary
But my impact will live forever

First the Man Takes the Drink, Then the Drink Takes the Man

This spirit-eating liquid floods this sober body
Intoxicating pure intentions
Holding hostage, the true ruler of this avatar
For the devil's juice reconnects with the lower self
Like crabs in a bucket, I remain enclosed
I've seen great leaders fall victim to this potion
As this bottle touches my lips
I find myself being poured back in
Drowning in an everlasting cycle

Have you ever had advice from someone, and it just went in one ear and out the other?

But then, as time goes on, the universe puts you in a situation where you have no choice but to learn the hard way.

Then you remember the advice they gave you and wish you had utilised it.

I've been on both sides of the fence. There have been times when I learned the hard way and then wished I had listened to the advice given. But I also think, if I didn't go through the lesson, then I wouldn't value the teachings.

I've also given them advice, watch people fall, and then return to me wishing they'd listened.

What I've learned is that you can take a horse to water but can't make it drink. You can guide someone onto the path and help them, but really, they need to experience it for themselves in order to grow.

We're all on our own journeys. Sometimes, we may have found another route that helped us progress quicker and want to share that. We need to know that we can't force those around us to walk the same way we did, for they have their own path and need to learn in their own way.

So don't take it to heart when you give someone advice and they ignore it. Let's be honest, we've all done it ourselves before. If we didn't ignore their advice, we probably wouldn't be who we are today, for the lessons stuck with us for a lifetime.

Random Thought

Who do you follow when the one who leads you falls astray?

Throw away your old keys
They won't unlock the doors on your new path

Afterword

I hope that after reading this,
my gibberish makes sense to you.

That my thoughts and feelings translated into
a language that resonated with your soul.
I hope you can relate to the pain, the love and all
the mess in between.

Most importantly I hope these words made you feel understood.

I encourage you all to write the poetic gibberish that comes to
your mind. Whether the poetry makes
sense or not, it doesn't matter, because it makes sense to you.

Poetry can be one word, 10 lines or a thousand lines.
There is no right or wrong. If it speaks to your soul,
write it down.

Express your thoughts and feelings,
cause if we don't
they'll eat us alive.

I'm no poet,
this isn't a poetry book.
It's just a visual insight into the pages of my chaotic mind.

If you understood me,
Thank you

I hope one day to hear your poetic gibberish.

Your Poetic Gibberish

All writers were once readers
And all readers have a story, a story
that's unique to them.

I encourage you to write your story, not to publish it,
but for you, for your heart, for your soul.

Write your story in the words that come to you
Just like I did in this book.

The next two pages are dedicated to your poetic gibberish.
Whether that be one word, a few rhymes or an entire story.
Let it be a reminder for you. A message that you can go
back to a look at when life's getting the upper hand.

A few topic ideas if you're unsure:

Childhood memory
First love
Heartbreak
Overcoming hurdles
A message to the old you or the future you

Be the foundation for your future self.

About the Author

I'm Karum Cheema, a 23-year-old still figuring things out on this rollercoaster called life. During the day, I work in the TV industry as a camera assistant/operator. But when the cameras stop rolling, I'm constantly looking for ways to express my creativity.

I've always thought of myself as a creative person. Sometimes I try and do so many different creative endeavours that I struggle to find the one that's fit for me. I've made music to try and help connect with people and although it was fun, I felt that I couldn't convey the message I wanted to get across authentically. That's why I turned to poetry. It was raw.

One of my biggest personal achievements and another one of my business endeavours is my clothing brand, *Rich Minds*. It's a brand driven by the ethos of self-growth and inner healing. Through my brand, I aim to be a catalyst for transformation, helping to guide people in finding the key within themselves to unlock their full potential.

I guess I'm just someone trying to spread some love and make the world a better place. Writing this book wasn't easy; I was scared about sharing my thoughts and feelings. But then, I realised life's too short for fears. If I want to make a difference, I have to walk the talk, right?

I mean sometimes I think I sound like a philosopher or something, but half the time what I say makes sense in my head, but doesn't make sense to others, probably like this section I'm writing now. But that's how poetic gibberish was born.

I hope my words strike a chord with you and maybe, just maybe, one of my poems speaks to your heart in a way that matters.